ART REVOLUTIONS

CUBISM

Linda Bolton

PETER BEDRICK BOOKS
NTC/Contemporary Publishing Group
NEW YORK

This American edition published 2000 by Peter Bedrick Books,
a division of NTC/Contemporary Publishing Group, Inc.,
4255 West Touhy Avenue, Lincolnwood (Chicago),
Illinois 60646-1975 U.S.A.

First published in Great Britain in 2000 by Belitha Press Limited,
London House, Great Eastern Wharf, Parkgate Road, London SW11 4NQ

Editor Susie Brooks
Designer Helen James
Picture Researcher Diana Morris
Educational Consultant Hester Collicutt
Consultants for US Edition Nathaniel Harris, Ruth Nason

Printed in China

International Standard Book Number: 0-87226-613-3

Library of Congress Cataloging-in-Publication data
is available from the United States Library of Congress.

00 01 02 03   15 14 13 12 11 10 9 8 7 6 5 4 3 2 1

Picture Credits:

Front cover: Jean Metzinger, The Cat, c. 1915. Private Collection. Photo Bridgeman Art Library. © DACS, London. 1: Albert Gleizes, The Clowns, 1917. Private Collection. Photo Giraudon/Bridgeman Art Library. © DACS, London. 4: Paul Cézanne, Le Lac d'Annecy, 1896. Courtauld Institute Galleries, London. Photo Bridgeman Art Library. 5: Fernand Léger, Mechanical Elements, 1918–23, Kunstmuseum, Basle. Photo Peter Willi/Bridgeman Art Library. © DACS, London. 6: Eadweard Muybridge, Athlete Running. Photographed synchronously from two points of view, 1887. Photo AKG London. 7t: Bakuba mask from Central Africa. British Museum, London. Photo Bridgeman Art Library. 7b: Pablo Picasso, Les Demoiselles d'Avignon, 1907. Museum of Modern Art, New York. Acquired through the Lillie P. Bliss Bequest. Photo © 1999 Museum of Modern Art, New York. © Succession Picasso, Paris/DACS, London. 8: Pablo Picasso, The Factory at the Village of Horta de Ebro, 1909. Hermitage, St. Petersburg. Photo Bridgeman Art Library. © Succession Picasso, Paris/ DACS London. 9t: Pablo Picasso, Ma Jolie, 1911–12. Museum of Modern Art, New York. Acquired through the Lillie P. Bliss Bequest. Photo © Museum of Modern Art, New York. © Succession Picasso, Paris/DACS, London. 9b: Pablo Picasso, Harlequin, 1915. Museum of Modern Art, New York. Acquired through the Lillie P. Bliss Bequest. Photo © Museum of Modern Art, New York. © Succession Picasso, Paris/DACS, London. 10: Georges Braque, Viaduct and Houses at L'Estaque, 1908. Musée National d'Art Moderne, Paris. Photo Peter Willi/ Bridgeman Art Library. © DACS, London. 11t: Georges Braque, The Sacré-Coeur of Montmartre, 1910. Donation Geneviève and Jean Masurel, 1979, Musée d'Art Moderne de Lille Métropole, Villeneuve d'Ascq. Photograph Muriel Anssens. © DACS, London. 11b: Georges Braque, Still Life with Violin and Pitcher, 1910. Offentliche Kunstsammlung, Basle. Photo Peter Willi/Bridgeman Art Library. © DACS, London. 12: Fernand Léger, Soldiers Playing Cards, 1917. Kroller-Müller Museum, Otterlo. © DACS, London. 13t: Fernand Léger, The Town, (1st stage), 1919. Galerie Daniel Malingue, Paris. Photo Bridgeman Art Library. 13b: Fernand Léger, The Tugboats, 1920. Musée de Grenoble. Photo Peter Willi/Bridgeman Art Library. © DACS, London. 14: Juan Gris, Portrait of Picasso, 1912. Art Institute of Chicago. Photo Lauros-Giraudon/Superstock. 15t: Juan Gris, Fantomas, 1915. Chester Dale Fund. National Gallery of Art,

Washington, D.C. 15b: Juan Gris, Landscape at Céret, 1913. Moderna Museet, Stockholm. 16: Robert Delaunay, The Eiffel Tower, 1910. Kunstmuseum, Basle. Photo AKG London. © L & M Services, Amsterdam. 17t: Robert Delaunay, Homage to Blériot, 1914. Kunstmuseum, Basle. Photo AKG London. © L & M Services, Amsterdam. 17b: Robert Delaunay, Window, Study for "Two Windows", 1912. Musée National d'Art Moderne, Paris. Photo Peter Willi-Artothek. © L & M Services, Amsterdam. 18: Albert Gleizes, Landscape, 1911. Musée National d'Art Moderne, Paris. Photo Peter Willi/Bridgeman Art Library. © DACS, London. 19t: Albert Gleizes, The Bridges of Paris, 1912. Museum Moderner Kunst, Stiftung Ludwig, Vienna. © DACS, London. 19b: Albert Gleizes, The Clowns, 1917. Private Collection. Photo Giraudon/Bridgeman Art Library. © DACS, London. 20: Jean Metzinger, The Cat, c. 1915. Private Collection. Photo Bridgeman Art Library. © DACS, London. 21t: Jean Metzinger, Tea Time (Woman with Teaspoon), 1911. Philadelphia Museum of Art. Photo Graydon Wood. © DACS, London. 21b: Jean Metzinger, The Knitter, 1919. Musée National d'Art Moderne, Paris. Photo Peter Willi/Bridgeman Art Library. © DACS, London. 22: Roger de La Fresnaye, Le Cuirassier, 1910–11. Musée National d'Art Moderne, Paris. 23: Roger de La Fresnaye, The Conquest of the Air, 1913. Museum of Modern Art, New York. Mrs. Simon Guggenheim Fund. Photo © 1999 Museum of Modern Art, New York. 24: Marcel Duchamp, Nude Descending a Staircase, No. 2, 1912. Philadelphia Museum of Art. Photo AKG London. © DACS, London. 25: Marcel Duchamp, Portrait of Chess Players, 1911. Philadelphia Museum of Art, Louise & Walter Arensberg Collection. Photo Bridgeman Art Library. © DACS, London. 26: Jacques Villon, Young Woman, 1912. Philadelphia Museum of Art, Louise & Walter Arensberg Collection. © DACS, London. 27: Jacques Villon, A Woman, 1913. Private Collection. Photo Bridgeman Art Library. © DACS, London. 28t: Gino Severini, Blue Dancer, 1912. Mattioli Collection, Milan. Photo Bridgeman Art Library. © DACS, London. 28b: Natalia Goncharova, The Cyclist, 1913. The Hermitage, St. Petersburg. Photo Bridgeman Art Library. 29t: Umberto Boccioni, Unique Forms of Continuity in Space, 1913. Mattioli Collection, Milan. Photo Bridgeman Art Library. 29b: Kasimir Malevich, The Aviator, 1914. The Hermitage, St. Petersburg. Photo Bridgeman Art Library.

CONTENTS

Useful words are explained on page 30.

CUBIST CLUES

Between 1908 and 1914, an art revolution took place in France, led by Pablo Picasso and Georges Braque. The Cubists created works in which objects and people were broken up and rearranged like geometric forms. This went against the entire tradition of western art. The Cubists were pioneers of the experimental arts of the twentieth century.

For centuries, most artists tried to capture exactly how things looked. Paintings were like photos of the real world. But, by about 1900, some artists were experimenting, for example by using non-realistic colors to convey feelings.

The Cubists went much further than this. They broke their subjects down into fragments and facets, and then rearranged the parts. These parts might be multiplied and seen from different points of view, like a side and frontal view of an eye.

Cubism was born in Paris, the center of the art world around 1900. The cofounders of Cubism were a French painter, Braque, and the Spanish artist Picasso. Braque was deeply influenced by an older French painter, Cézanne, who wrote that "All nature is made up of the cone, the cylinder, and the sphere." The name Cubism comes from the cube forms in some of Braque's paintings.

Cubist art did not pretend to be a copy of a real scene. Instead of creating an illusion that painted images were three-dimensional, the Cubists emphasized the flat picture surface, sometimes even sticking objects onto it. Cubists wanted people to accept that a work of art was a separate, artificial creation. It was something brand new, not just a mirror of the world outside it.

PAUL CÉZANNE
Lake at Annecy

1896, oil paint on canvas

The cones, cylinders, and spheres that Cézanne spoke of are not always obvious in his own paintings. But everything in this picture, even the reflections on the water, is strong and solid. Cézanne has organized his colors into blocks, balancing lights and darks. He has simplified nature, creating a calm and orderly image.

FERNAND LÉGER
Mechanical Elements

1918–23, oil paint on canvas

The Cubists admired the solid structure of Cézanne's art. Léger said, "Cézanne taught me to love forms and volumes. He made me concentrate on drawing." Here Léger has abandoned realism, using geometric shapes and plain, bright colors to create a modern image like chaotic machinery at work.

The idea that a work can be independent of reality has influenced the entire history of art – which is what makes Cubism so important. Once they were not trying to copy reality, the Cubists found new ways to make the surfaces of their pictures more interesting. The most important of these techniques, collage and papier collé, are described later in this book.

Fascinated by rearranging forms, Braque and Picasso applied their revolutionary approach to traditional subjects and even painted in quiet colors in order to concentrate on form. But, by 1912, other artists had taken up Cubism, using bright colors and tackling modern subjects. Though interrupted by World War I, Cubism went on to influence modern art everywhere.

EADWEARD MUYBRIDGE
Athlete Running

1887, photographic sequence

This is a series of pictures taken by the American photographer Eadweard Muybridge. He made sets of photos showing how people actually moved. These enabled artists to see figures from many angles and in many positions. They influenced artists such as Marcel Duchamp (page 24).

BAKUBA MASK from Central Africa

c. 1900, wood

Many Cubist painters were influenced by African art. They thought that "primitive" works were as powerful in their way as most western paintings and sculptures. Picasso collected African masks such as this one. He liked their bold shapes and patterning and their raw energy. He admired their strength and unfamiliar beauty, which affected his own development.

PABLO PICASSO
Les Demoiselles d'Avignon

1907, oil paint on canvas

This painting is often seen as the starting point of Cubism – and of modern art itself. The faces of the two women on the right show how much Picasso was influenced by African carvings. He deliberately made his figures look distorted and primitive. The painting was so revolutionary that, for a long while, Picasso did not show it even to his most daring artistic friends. Turn the page to see where he went from there!

PABLO PICASSO 1881–1973

"I paint forms as I think them, not as I see them."

Pablo Picasso is probably the most famous artist of the twentieth century. He was born in Spain, where he began his training as an artist. He was the son of an art teacher, and could draw and paint brilliantly from early boyhood.

At age nineteen, Picasso moved to Paris, where he experimented with many art styles. He soon took an interest in African and ancient Spanish art, as well as the paintings of Paul Cézanne. These led him to pioneer the revolutionary Cubist style.

The Factory at the Village of Horta

1909, oil paint on canvas

Picasso revisited Spain many times during his first few years of living in Paris. He missed his native country and its hot, sunny weather. It was on a visit to Spain in the summer of 1909 that he painted this factory scene. The buildings, palm trees, and clouds are reduced to simple geometric forms. The contrasting shades of orange and gray make the blocklike shapes stand out in different ways. The three-dimensional effect Picasso achieved is like that of a gemstone – an object with many facets.

Ma Jolie

1911–12, oil paint on canvas

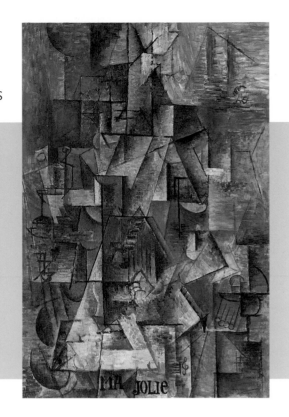

The title of this painting means "my pretty one" in French. It is a portrait of a woman known as Eva, with whom Picasso had fallen in love. The outline of a woman can just about be seen, but more obvious are some musical elements. *Ma Jolie* was the title of a song that was popular in 1911, and Picasso has actually painted it onto the canvas. A treble clef sign makes us think of music, and other shapes in the picture look like parts of a guitar. But this amazingly composed work is not really a picture *of* something: it is simply a picture.

INVENTING COLLAGE

If the Cubists were not trying to copy reality, why should they always use traditional oil paints? In 1912, Picasso made art history by gluing a piece of oilcloth onto his canvas. Arranging and sticking down objects – collage – became a new weapon in the artist's armory.

Harlequin

1915, oil paint on canvas

Picasso said this painting was the best he had ever done. It is different from his earlier Cubist works. Everything is simplified, looking like a series of flat, cut-out shapes. A harlequin is a clown who wears a checkered costume. Here, the harlequin is a diamond-patterned rectangle with a slice cut out of it to form two legs. The head and neck are like a ball on a stick, with a circle representing an eye. Picasso had given up dull colors and complicated arrangements, but there is still a strong emphasis on geometric shapes.

GEORGES BRAQUE 1882–1963

"Picasso and I were like mountaineers roped together."

Georges Braque learned to paint in his family's decorating firm. Later he turned to fine art and moved to Paris, where he worked so closely with Picasso that sometimes their work was hard to tell apart. Later, even the artists themselves struggled to remember who had painted what!

In 1914, Braque joined the French army to fight in World War I. Afterward, he and Picasso were less close. Picasso experimented with new styles as well as sometimes returning to Cubism. His originality made him world-famous. Braque developed his pre-war ideas, also much admired.

Viaduct and Houses at L'Estaque

1908, oil paint on canvas

The painter Henri Matisse (1869–1954) spoke of this painting as being entirely made up of little cubes. The southern French landscape is not shown realistically, but is reduced to simple shapes. It is clear that Braque was influenced by Paul Cézanne (1839–1906), who had lived and worked in this part of France. There are also similarities between this work by Braque and Picasso's *Factory at the Village of Horta* (page 8), painted in 1909.

The Sacré-Coeur

1910, oil paint on canvas

The Sacré-Coeur is a famous hilltop church in Paris. Like the Eiffel Tower, it can be seen from many places in the city below. It is one of the great Parisian landmarks. Here we can see the domes of the church at the top of the painting. The building is cut up into geometric shapes that overlap and interlock. The bold patches of steely sky appear as solid as the stone itself. By using dull grays and browns Braque directs our attention to the forms, rather than distracting us with bright colors.

NEW IDEAS

In 1911, Braque began to stencil words onto his canvases. He painted some areas so that they looked like wood graining. Later, he followed Picasso's invention of collage with papier collé pictures – glued-down paper cut-outs.

Still Life with Violin and Pitcher

1910, oil paint on canvas

Braque and Picasso painted many still lifes of musical instruments, and also of bottles, glasses, and pitchers. The things that stand out most clearly in this picture are the strings and body of a violin. It looks as if it has been broken and rearranged, or is being viewed through rippled glass. The pitcher and other objects merge into a mass of faceted shapes. Unlike a realistic picture, Braque's still life gives equal importance to every area of the canvas.

FERNAND LÉGER

1881–1955

The French artist Fernand Léger trained as an architect before becoming a painter. He joined the Cubists in 1909, though he painted more colorfully than Picasso and Braque. His simplified, cylindrical forms led some people to call him a "tubist" rather than a Cubist!

Léger fought in World War I. His experience of comradeship made him want to produce a popular art, closer to people's lives than his pre-war work. It was still often Cubist in arrangement, but filled with dynamic energy and concerned with modern industry and city life.

Soldiers Playing Cards

1917, oil paint on canvas

Léger's card players are like robots. They have thick, regular fingers on cone-shaped hands, which seem to rotate on cylindrical arms. Their spines are built up from jointed angular blocks, like pointed chunks of metal. Everything in the painting looks as if it could be part of a machine. But Léger reminds us that these are human figures by showing them smoking pipes and playing cards. Repeated shapes give a sense of movement, reflecting the lively action of the game.

The Town
1919, oil paint on canvas

This is an imaginative view of a busy town. Léger has painted aspects of the modern world in a modern way. We can see the criss-cross grid shape of a pylon in the top right corner, and what looks like a factory, bottom left. Clouds of smoke, like transparent bubbles, seem to emerge from a white smokestack in the center. The shape running up the left side of the picture looks like the edge of a tall building. It is as if we are looking down at the town from the window of an upper story.

EVERYDAY BALLET
In 1923–24 Léger produced a movie called *Le Ballet Mécanique*, with photography by Man Ray. It has no plot and shows everyday objects in rhythmic movement.

Tugboats
1920, oil paint on canvas

We may not immediately see Léger's tugboats. More recognizable are three figures, a ladder, and a dog. All the abstract shapes around them have something to do with boats in a port. The tubes remind us of smokestacks, the circles of portholes. Léger has not painted a view of a port, but a collection of shapes that echo the geometric forms of tugboats and a pier.

JUAN GRIS 1887–1927

"I try to make abstract things become real."

Like Picasso, Juan Gris was born in Spain. He began working as a magazine illustrator in Madrid before moving to Paris, where he continued making humorous pictures for political journals. After seeing the work of Picasso and Braque, he took up painting and worked in the Cubist style.

Gris was interested in science and engineering and his paintings show this in their carefully structured compositions. He built up images from abstract shapes, and often used collage to help him achieve different effects. Many other Cubists were inspired by his ideas.

Portrait of Picasso

1912, oil paint on canvas

Gris lived near Picasso in Paris, where he painted this portrait. Through the maze of geometric shapes you can make out the figure of Picasso, seated in a chair. In one hand he holds an artist's palette. You cannot see his features clearly, and his body and the armchair tend to merge. The image is made up of many fragments, all of them shaded as if they are separate forms. The picture is hardly a portrait, but is fascinating in its shifting dynamic patterns.

Still Life (Fantomas)
1915, oil paint on canvas

We can recognize a number of objects in this painting, overlapping and merging in a way that would be impossible in reality. We can pick out a paperback thriller with the title *Fantomas* (meaning "Ghosts"), a pipe, a newspaper, a wood panel, and a tiled floor. All these objects look fragmented. Parts of some things seem to have disappeared. And, in a different style, a wine glass, fruit, and table are painted in white outline over or in among the solid-looking objects.

STILL LIFE
A still life is a picture filled with unmoving objects. Unlike a living model or a changing landscape, a still life can be arranged exactly as the artist wants. Still life was particularly suitable for the Cubists' complex paintings and collages.

Landscape at Céret
1913, oil paint on canvas

Here we see a bright landscape, but not in its original form. The impression we get is of a poster that has been cut up and rearranged. Gris has put together different viewpoints on the same plane. He shows us roof tiles seen from above, and walls and trees seen from the side. Intense, bright colors suggest the blazing heat of the sun. Everything is simplified and fragmented. It is like a memory of the place.

ROBERT DELAUNAY

1885–1941

"I wanted to put different sides next to each other."

Robert Delaunay was born in Paris. He trained as a theatrical decorator before becoming a painter. Delaunay loved the color and pace of modern city life. He wanted to paint this energy and not simply show what the streets looked like.

Delaunay's art is based on color, light, rhythm and movement. He wanted his paintings to make music for the eyes. The poet and art critic Apollinaire named his style Orphic Cubism (from the musician Orpheus in Greek mythology).

The Eiffel Tower
1910, oil paint on canvas

Delaunay painted around thirty pictures of the Eiffel Tower. This great Paris landmark was built in 1889 for an international exhibition held in the city. It was a symbol of the triumph of modern engineering and became an emblem of France itself. Delaunay admired the eye-catching structure of the Tower and here he conveys the excitement he felt when he saw it. The bright, light, vivid colors and fragmented forms suggest energy and life. The Tower itself almost seems to leap around!

Homage to Blériot

1914, oil paint on canvas

Louis Blériot (1872-1936) made the first flight across the sea from France to England. You can see a propeller on the left of this painting, and, at the top, a biplane soaring over the Eiffel Tower. Propeller shapes are repeated throughout the picture, as are colored discs. Delaunay saw these discs as symbols of the energy and light he associated with the fast-changing modern world.

COLOR MAGIC

Delaunay found that areas of pure color could be placed side by side, with often dazzling effects. He also learned how to use color alone to create an impression of movement. In 1912, he became the first French artist to paint completely abstract pictures.

For this painting, Delaunay did not work from an actual view through a window, but from an image on a postcard of the Eiffel Tower, as seen from another Paris landmark, the Arc de Triomphe. When you look closely, you can make out the Tower, but it seems to be dissolved in a mass of colored shapes. Delaunay suggests the presence of buildings, but nothing is solid here. Light and color take over, giving us an impression of Paris.

Window, Study for "Two Windows"

1912, oil paint on canvas

ALBERT GLEIZES 1881–1953

Albert Gleizes was born in Paris. He worked as an industrial designer before becoming a painter. Influenced by Braque and Picasso, he began not only to paint in the Cubist style, but also to write about it. With the French painter Jean Metzinger, he wrote *Cubism*, the first book to be published about the movement.

After serving in the French army during World War I, Gleizes traveled to the USA where he exhibited his work. While there, he became very religious. He spent the rest of his life trying to create a Christian form of modern art.

Landscape
1911, oil paint on canvas

Here we see a gray figure who seems to step from a path into a landscape made up of hard, angular shapes. The path bears left and disappears into the background, but Gleizes makes little use of traditional perspective techniques to suggest distance. There is no easily identifiable horizon, and only a few areas of pale color hint that any of the trees, buildings, and clouds are far away. The invention of photography made artists less interested in creating an illusion of reality. Gleizes has created a powerful composition, filled with solid forms that seem to press up against the picture surface.

TWO CUBISMS
Cubism began with Picasso and Braque. In their "Analytical Cubism," forms were broken down. In the second phase, "Synthetic Cubism," Gleizes and others put more stress on human images and used brighter colors.

18

The Bridges of Paris

1912, oil paint on canvas

Like many Cubist landscapes, this painting looks as if it has been created by rearranging the pieces of a cut-up picture. The bridges, which are usually seen in line over the River Seine, appear here in fragmented pieces, placed all over the scene. You can see some arches among buildings, streets, clouds, and trees. Similar to paintings by Picasso and Braque, this is an ingenious composition.

The Clowns

1917, oil paint on canvas

In this bright and lively painting, two clowns can be seen amid a swirl of intersecting circles. These spiraling shapes remind us of cartwheels and somersaults – the acrobatics that clowns might perform in a circus ring. Gleizes creates a sense of movement, especially of things spinning. The solid color in the central part of the painting seems to rotate. By contrast, broken outlines show the clowns' legs and feet at rest but about to move. So Gleizes cleverly suggests both stillness and movement.

19

JEAN METZINGER 1883–1956

Jean Metzinger was born and studied art in Nantes in France. After moving to Paris, he met the other Cubists, and often visited Picasso's studio. He showed his work in Cubist exhibitions, and he and Gleizes wrote the first book on Cubism.

Besides this book (1912), Metzinger also published magazine articles on modern painting. After serving in the army in World War I, he returned to work in Paris. His paintings are full of flat, geometric shapes, often in bright colors.

The Cat

1915, oil paint on canvas

In this painting we see the cat's face both from the side and from the front. This makes it seem as if the animal is moving its head, turning to play with the ball of wool by its back paw. The shape of the cat has been simplified. Its back leg has a zigzag outline, giving the impression that it is bending in a quick, agile movement. The angular gray shadow behind this leg suggests that the cat has just moved from this space. Metzinger has simplified colors, tones, and textures so that the image looks flat, but it is full of life and movement.

Tea Time

1911, oil paint on board

Here a woman is sitting at a table, with one hand holding a spoon and the other touching a cup and saucer. Again, Metzinger has skillfully brought together objects seen from different viewpoints. One half of the cup and saucer is shown from the side, and the other from above. Similarly, one of the woman's eyes is seen from the front, and the other from the side. Her shoulders merge into the background, which is blocked in with typical Cubist solidity.

The Knitter

1919, oil paint on canvas

AVANT-GARDE ART

This phrase is often used in discussions of modern art. It means "advanced guard" and was first applied to soldiers. Then, about 1910 – the Cubist era – it was used of art that was ahead of public taste. There have been many avant-garde movements.

This is a striking example of the way in which the Cubists managed to combine a more or less recognizable image with a flat pattern made up of many different parts. On one level this is obviously a seated woman knitting at a table. It is easy to identify the woman's hands, her body, the knitting itself, and the chair she sits on. Yet, the more you look, the more you can see that Metzinger has built up the image from a series of flat, overlapping shapes. The sharply separated pieces look almost like cards that have been slotted together at different angles.

ROGER DE LA FRESNAYE

"Each object gradually becomes part of the painting."

Born at Le Mans in France, La Fresnaye was artistically gifted from childhood. Around 1910, he met the Cubists, and adopted their style.

He used geometric shapes in his work, but his images are more naturalistic and less fragmented than those in many Cubist works.

Le Cuirassier
1910–11, oil paint on canvas

The dramatic figure of the soldier stretches right across this huge painting, from top to bottom and from left to right. The power of the armed warrior is emphasized by the control he shows over his straining horse, whose reins he clasps in his right hand. The background is hazily outlined, conveying the smoke and confusion of battle. But we can just see the red helmets of two soldiers, and two French flags flying.

22

The Conquest of the Air

1913, oil paint on canvas

In this painting, the artist is talking to his brother, Henri, who was the director of an aircraft factory. They seem to be floating above the houses as they discuss the conquest of the air. The balloon high above is a reminder that the French Montgolfier brothers had been the first humans to take to the skies, with a hot-air balloon, in 1783. In 1903, the Wright brothers in the USA flew the first powered plane. But, when this picture was painted, the most recent triumph of all was Blériot's flight (see page 17). So La Fresnaye has patriotically put in a French flag.

MARCEL DUCHAMP 1887–1968

"We paint because we want to be free."

Marcel Duchamp was born in Normandy in France. He was one of six children, four of whom became famous artists. His eldest brother Gaston was another Cubist, known as Jacques Villon (see page 26).

Marcel first trained as a librarian and then as an illustrator before becoming a painter. He experimented with a number of styles, including Cubism, and soon turned his back completely on traditional painting. Duchamp was a true revolutionary in the art world.

"An explosion in a shingle factory" was how one critic described this painting when he saw it exhibited at the Armory Show in New York in 1913. The flurry of angular brown shapes was totally unlike anything anyone had seen before. If you look closely, you can see how Duchamp learned from Muybridge's photographs of people moving (see page 6). He has painted a figure rushing downstairs by showing every stage of the movement. We do not see the figure clearly, but the repeated forms make us feel its speed.

Nude Descending a Staircase No. 2

1912, oil paint on canvas

Portrait of
Chess Players
1911, oil paint on canvas

Marcel Duchamp was an avid chess player – in fact, for long periods, he preferred playing chess to creating works of art! Here he shows two figures in the middle of a game. They are not hard to pick out, though their forms are broken up and the colors are soft. The players are obviously deep in thought. The figure on the right is resting an arm on a table and a hand against his chin. The other player holds a pawn, and between the heads of the two figures we can see more chess pieces and the chessboard.

ARTIST OR JOKER?
Duchamp invented the ready-made, an artwork that was really a manufactured object. In 1913, he showed a bicycle wheel mounted on a kitchen stool. In 1919, he produced his version of the famous female portrait of *Mona Lisa* – giving her a mustache and beard.

JACQUES VILLON 1875–1963

Like his brother, Marcel Duchamp (page 24), Villon worked as an illustrator before turning to fine art. He was a great thinker and loved math, which he saw as the base for Cubist art.

Villon formed a group of artists called the *Section d'Or* (Golden Square), who met in his studio and showed their work together. They included Léger, Delaunay, Duchamp, Gris, Gleizes, and Metzinger.

Young Woman

1912, oil paint on canvas

This dazzling kaleidoscope of colors could easily be taken as a purely abstract painting. However, the title makes us look harder. We can identify the young woman, though her outline is shifting and uncertain. This, along with the stripes and play of colors in the background, creates a strong impression of energy and movement. As in all the best Cubist paintings, every area of the canvas is fully alive.

A Woman

1913, oil paint on canvas

In contrast to the painting on page 26, this is obviously a portrait. The woman's face is clearly shown, and she looks like an individual, not a generalized image. But this is still a Cubist work, with geometric patterns knitting together the picture surface. The shapes in the background continue into the woman's hair, and her clothes are shown as large, irregular diamonds. Only her face is free from geometric patterning, as if Villon is giving the human element a special place.

Artists in many countries soon took up Cubism. Often they developed new styles, using Cubist ideas for somewhat different purposes. Among these styles were Futurism in Italy and Constructivism in Russia. A few examples are shown on these two pages.

GINO SEVERINI
Blue Dancer

1912, oil paint on canvas

Italian Futurists like Severini (1883–1966) loved speed, modernity, and machinery. This painting of a dancer in a blue dress is lively and energetic. Forms are fragmented and repeated to give a sense of rhythm and rapid movement.

NATALIA GONCHAROVA
The Cyclist

1913, oil paint on canvas

Goncharova (1881–1962) was a Russian artist. Here, the cyclist is almost transparent, merging with roadside posters and cobblestones. He seems to whizz past.

UMBERTO BOCCIONI
Unique Forms of Continuity in Space
1913, bronze

Both painter and sculptor, the Futurist Boccioni (1882–1916) showed how Cubism could be applied to three-dimensional work. This sculpture looks like a shiny, metallic robot moving powerfully through space.

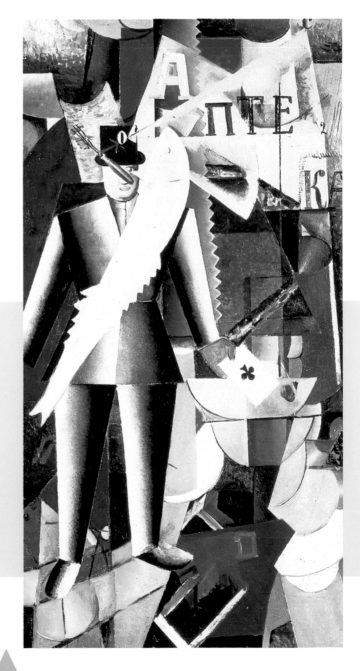

KASIMIR MALEVICH
The Aviator
1914, oil paint on canvas

This work by Russian artist Malevich (1878–1935) shows an aviator with a tubular metallic body, somewhat similar to Léger's figures. The aviator is surrounded by an amazing variety of overlapping shapes, which are not easy to identify. The playing card in the man's hand, the fork beside his head, and the random lettering add to the mystery.

abstract art Art that does not show images from the real world. It relies on shapes, textures, and colors to interest the viewer.

Analytical Cubism A name given to the first phase of Cubism (1909–11), in which artists took apart their subjects, analyzed the pieces, and rearranged them in a new composition. (See Synthetic Cubism, below.)

Armory Show A big modern art exhibition held in New York in 1913. It featured the work of the Cubists, and spread the style to the USA.

canvas A strong fabric on which artists paint.

collage A collection of materials, such as paper, fabric, and photos, stuck onto a background.

composition The way a work of art is arranged.

Constructivism An art movement in Russia that was influenced by the Cubist style. The Constructivists were interested in geometric shapes. Often their work is quite abstract.

fine art Art that is not made for any practical purpose or to convey any commercial message.

fragmented Broken into many pieces.

Futurism An art movement in Italy that was influenced by Cubism. Like the Cubists, the Futurists were interested in the machine age and the city, and particularly in dynamic movement.

harlequin A comic theatrical character, usually shown wearing a black mask and a diamond-patterned costume. Its geometric form made the harlequin a favorite subject for the Cubists.

image A picture or idea.

industrial designer Someone who designs products to be manufactured in a factory.

movement A style or period of art.

Orphic Cubism A term invented by the poet and art critic Guillaume Apollinaire (1880–1918) to describe the color-dominated form of Cubism developed by Delaunay.

papier collé Paper pieces pasted down to make a picture.

perspective A system used in painting and drawing to create an illusion of depth and space. Scenes drawn in perspective appear to recede into the distance, just as real scenes do.

plane A flat surface.

retrospective Looking backward. A retrospective exhibition looks back on an artist's life's work, often after his or her death.

Section d'Or *Section d'Or* is French. It means "Golden Section," a theory of artistic proportions. The name was used by the group of artists led by Jacques Villon. It was also the name of a magazine produced by the group and an exhibition of their work in 1912.

still life An arrangement of objects that cannot move, such as fruit, flowers, or bottles.

Synthetic Cubism A name given to the phase of Cubism (1912–14) that followed the Analytical phase. Instead of fragmenting objects, artists now brought together already existing things.

CUBIST TIMES

1895 First motion picture shown in a Paris theater by Lumière brothers.

1903 First manned plane flight achieved by Wright brothers, USA.

1906 Death of Paul Cézanne.

1907 Retrospective exhibition of Cézanne's paintings impresses many artists. Picasso studies African masks for first time. He paints *Les Demoiselles d'Avignon*.

1908 Comments of the art critic Louis Vauxcelles about some landscapes by Georges Braque give rise to the name Cubism.

1909 Louis Blériot makes first flight across English Channel.

1912 *Section d'Or* group is established. Members include Gleizes, Gris, La Fresnaye, Léger, Metzinger, and Villon. First Cubist exhibition in Paris. Gleizes and Metzinger publish *Du Cubisme*, the first book-length account of the movement.

1914 Outbreak of World War I. Braque, Gleizes, La Fresnaye, Léger, and Metzinger all serve.

1918 End of World War I.

FURTHER INFORMATION

Galleries to visit

There are many places where original Cubist paintings can be seen. Some of the largest collections are in the USA. The **Museum of Modern Art**, New York, houses Picasso's *Les Demoiselles d'Avignon* and many more, and the **Philadelphia Museum of Art** also has a number of examples.

In Paris, France, where Cubism was born, the **Musée Picasso** is dedicated to this revolutionary artist. In London, UK, the **Tate Gallery of Modern Art** has many Cubist works, particularly by Picasso and Braque, and the **Estorick Collection** has a small but fine gallery of paintings by the Italian Futurists.

Websites to browse

http://sunsite.org.uk/wm/paint/tl/20th/cubism/html

http://www.salford.ac.uk/modlang/ote/aditi/modart/html

htp://www.stockportmbe.gov.uk/pages

Books to read

Cézanne by Mike Venezia, from the *Getting to Know the World's Greatest Artists and Composers* series, Children's Press, 1998 (also a title on *Picasso*)

Cézanne from A to Z by Marie Sellier, Peter Bedrick Books, 1996

Picasso by Stefano Loria, from the *Masters of Art* series, Peter Bedrick Books, 1995

Picasso, Breaking the Rules of Art by David Spence, from the *Great Artists* series, Barrons, 1997

Understanding Modern Art by Monica Bohm-Duchen and Janet Cook, EDC Publications, 1992

What Makes a Picasso a Picasso? by Richard Mühlberger, Metropolitan Museum of Art, 1994

INDEX